Amazing Questions & Answers

Robot

Om Books International

Om Books International

Reprinted in 2025

Corporate & Editorial Office
A-12, Sector 64, Noida 201 301
Uttar Pradesh, India
Phone: +91 120 477 4100
Email: editorial@ombooks.com
Website: www.ombooksinternational.com

Sales Office
107, Ansari Road, Darya Ganj
New Delhi 110 002, India
Phone: +91 11 4000 9000
Email: sales@ombooks.com
Website: www.ombooks.com

ISBN: 978-93-52766-53-6

Printed in India

10 9 8 7 6 5 4

What can a robot do?

What?

Why?

How do robots move?

Why do robots have sensors?

How?

When?

When does a robot get tired?

CONTENTS

What?

What is a robot?

A machine! A robot is a mechanical device that can carry out a variety of simple and complex actions on a command. It can also act according to instructions programmed in advance. Robots are designed by engineers to perform difficult tasks easily and with greater accuracy.

Find out

In which country can you find the most number of robots?

Pocket fact

Robota!
The word 'robot' comes from a Czech word 'robota', which means 'hard work or dull work'.

What can a robot do?

A lot of tasks! Robots can do many different kinds of jobs, like helping doctors perform delicate surgeries, assemble big cars and tiny computer chips. Robots are also sent deep into the ocean or into space to explore things.

What are the basic things a robot needs to work automatically?

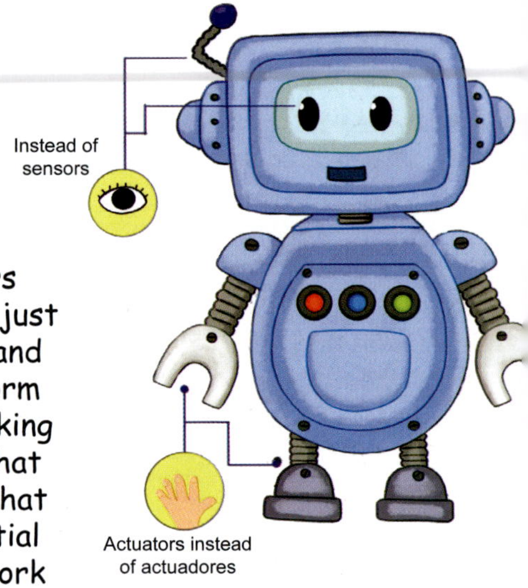

Sensors, Actuators and Program! The sensors help a robot to perceive the world around it just like our sense organs (eyes, ears, nose, skin and tongue). The actuators help a robot to perform actions such as moving, making faces and making sounds. A program is a set of instructions that that lets robots act on their own based on what it is sensing. A robot must have three essential parts- sensors, actuators and programs to work automatically.

Find out

What is a controller in a robot?

Pocket fact

So many sensors!

A robot can have a number of sensors depending on the task it performs. These can be to detect colours, temperature, light and so on!

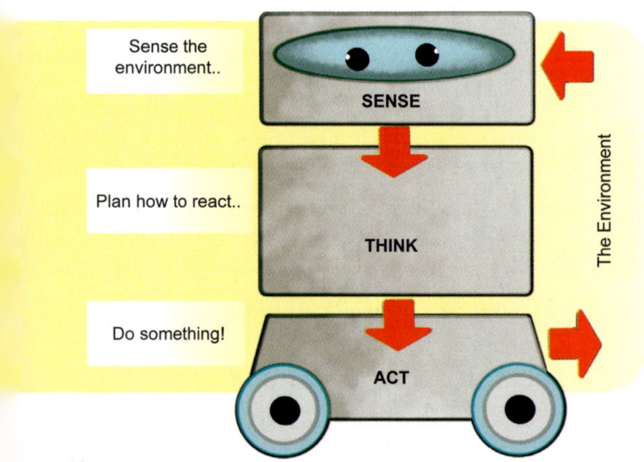

What is the Sense-Think-Act Cycle?

It is a decision-making process used by robots! A robot senses the world around it with the help of sensors. A robot cannot think like we do but its program helps it to plan how to react based on what it has sensed. Then the robot executes the action to be carried out i.e. it acts upon the world. This Sense-Think-Act Cycle is what makes robots different from other machines.

What are the different types of robots in use?

Many types! There are many ways we can define different types of robots. Based on their application and use, robots can be divided into eight types. These are industrial robots, domestic or household robots, medical robots, service robots, military robots, entertainment robots, space robots, and hobby and competition robots.

Find out

What is the study of robots called?

Pocket fact

Robots on Mars!

Two robots named Spirit and Opportunity were sent to Mars to explore the planet. They do much of their work alone, without commands from Earth because it takes a long time to send a signal from Earth to Mars.

What was the first known robot?

It was a mechanical dove! Yes, the first robot did not look like complex machines or human-like robots. It was mechanical doves. It was created in the 5th century BCE by a Greek mathematician and astronomer Archytas. He made a wooden dove worked with the helped of compressed air or steam. The dove could fly hundreds of feet into the air while tethered to the ground.

What is a humanoid robot?

A humanoid robot is a robot that resembles a human being's body structure. Such a robot has a torso, a head, two arms and two legs. Some humanoids also have eyes and mouth. A humanoid robot helps us to perform human tasks like scientific research, entertainment, in mines, personal assistance and greeting guests and visitors.

Find out

What does the word android mean?

Pocket fact

The First Humanoid Design!
The first design of a humanoid robot was made by Leonardo da Vinci in the year 1495.

What is an Android robot?

An Android is a humanoid robot that looks and acts like a human. But it is different from a humanoid because it has a body with a flesh-like resemblance just as humans. Android robots can use machines, tools and infrastructure. They can perform many tasks that humans can do.

What is a robonaut?

It is a humanoid robot! A robonaut is a NASA robot. It is designed to work in space or in high risk environments. It is made up of a torso, two arms, a head and two legs with end effectors. Robonaut is currently operated inside the International Space Station.

Pocket fact

In 2000!
NASA started working on the Robonaut project in 1996. The first version of the robot was created in 2000.

Find out

What does 'nano' mean?

What is a nanobot?

A very tiny robot! A nanobot or a nanorobot is such a small robot that you need a microscope to see it. It is used to perform specific tasks repeatedly and with accuracy at very small dimensions. Nanorobots are still being developed. They would be of great help in performing delicate surgery.

What were some of the early robots?

They were automata- moving machines driven by water, air or clockwork! These automatic machines have been designed by inventors since ancient times. For example: mechanical doves, the elephant clock Karakuri puppets. The elephant clock was designed by an Arab inventor al-Jazari in 1206. Karakuri puppets were mechanical dolls that could act out stories at the theatre.

Find out

What does the word 'Karakuri' mean?

Pocket fact

Electric Teeth!
The robot Eric could make blue sparks from its teeth by using electricity.

What was the first human-shaped robo

It was called Eric! Eric was the first British robot built in 1928. It was 7 feet tall and had armour that made it look like a knight. The inside of its body had many wires connected to motors. The wires helped it do different actions like stand, sit, turn left and right and wave its arms. Though Eric was able to sit and stand it could not move its legs to walk.

What were the first robots to make their own decisions?

They were two tortoises! An American scientist William Grey Walter designed two robot tortoises named Elmer and Elsie. They could react to their surroundings like real animals and make their own decisions.

Pocket fact

Shakey was named so because it was tall and had a tendency to shake!

Find out

In which year were Elmer and Elsie created?

What was the first robot that was able to think for itself?

It was called Shakey! Shakey was the first general-purpose mobile robot that could think for itself. It was developed at the Standford Research Institute, California. Shakey was a tall robot with an antenna for a radio link, sonar range finders, a television camera and bump detectors. It could look around a room using its camera and plan how to move without bumping into things using its bump detectors.

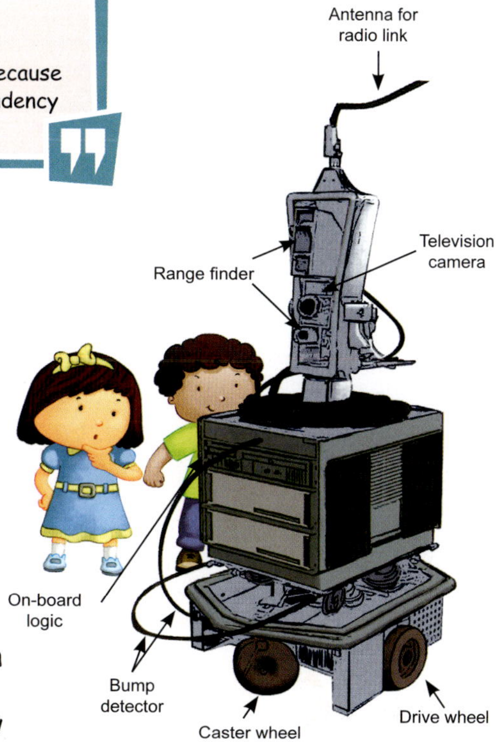

What is a Nao?

A robot that plays soccer and does lots more! Nao is a friendly human-like robot that was developed in France. It is a smart interactive robot that was programmed by roboticists to walk, talk and play RoboCup soccer! Robo has been continually been evolving since its invention. It can welcome guests and provide information in a variety of languages when placed at hotels!

Pocket fact

Robots at the Show!

The first show in the world with robots in the starring roles was held in 2013. NAO was a part of this "ROBOTS" show and charmed the audience.

Try this

In which year was SAFFIR invented?

What kind of robot is a SAFFIR?

A fire-fighting robot! SAFFIR was developed by TREC (a technology company in Virginia) and the U.S. Navy. It can see through smoke. Its main purpose is to assist sailors in fighting fires, controlling damage and carrying out inspections onboard ships.

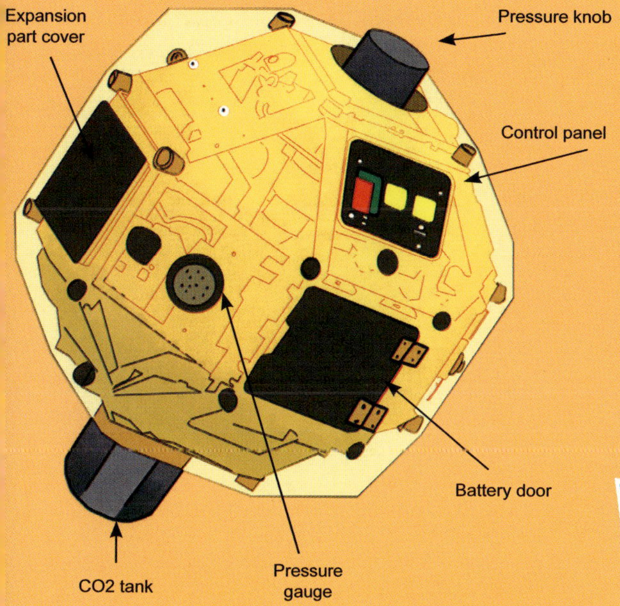

What work do SPHERES robots do?

They help astronauts in space! SPHERES are robots in the shape of spherical satellites that are free flying. SPHERES are used inside the International Space Station. They help in testing instructions for spacecraft that perform automated tasks.

Pocket fact

SPHERES robots are also used by students at Robotics competitions.

What are the special features of the KISMET robot?

It is an expressive robot that was designed to relate to people and learn from them. It was developed in the United States in late 1990s. KISMET has learnt about feelings. It can make faces to express happiness, sadness or surprise!

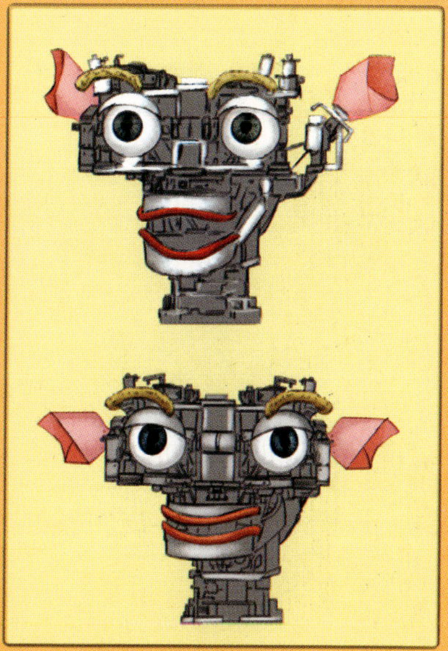

Find out

Can the KISMET robot speak?

What is a tracked robot?

A robot that moves on tracks instead of wheels! Robots with tracks are suitable for moving across uneven surfaces. They can move on ice, mud and even snow! Robots with track are designed to fight fires and travel in space.

Find out

What are caterpillar tracks?.

Flipper arms!

Tracked robots may also have flipper arms. They use these arms to climb stairs or obstacles that are a lot taller than them.

What are wheeled robots?

Robots that use wheels to move! Robots with wheels are fast to move, easier to build and program. They are also better controlled than other types of robots. But such robots can trip over bumpy ground. Robots with wheels are used to mow lawns, guard prisons and carry materials inside factories and hospitals.

What are legged robots used for?

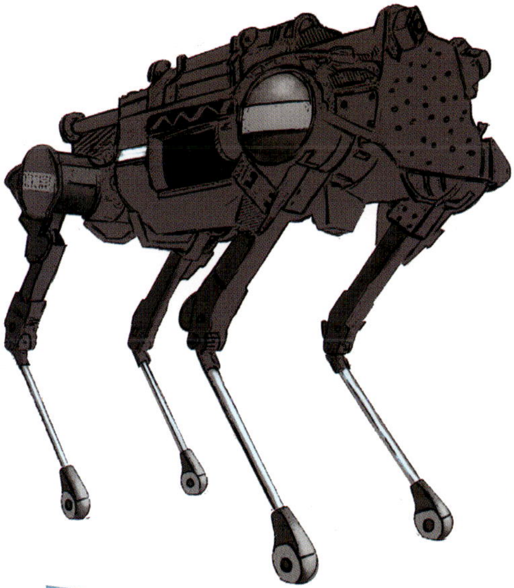

Legged robots are robots that use limbs to move around. They resemble humans or insects. Robots with legs are suitable to climb up walls or step over objects. Such robots are used in jobs like cleaning up chemical spills or exploring uneven surface of the ocean floor.

Find out

In which year was the Handle robot built?

The Big Dog!

The Big Dog is a four-legged robot that resembles a mule. It was created to help soldiers where vehicles can't be used to carry loads.

What are hybrid robots?

Robots that have both legs and wheels are called hybrid robots. Such robots can move fast because of wheels as well as walk and climb with their legs. The robot Handle built by a company called Boston Dynamics, is an example of a hybrid robot.

What is a snakebot?

It's a robot in the form of a snake! A robotic snake or snakebot moves from side to side like a snake. It has tiny cameras along its body to help us monitor what the robot snake sees. Such robots can climb trees and swim. They can be used to move through collapsed buildings after an earthquake where people can't enter.

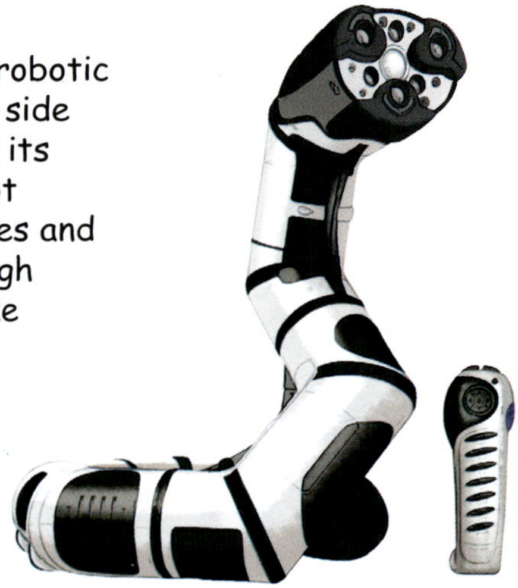

Find out

How much does the Cyro weigh?

What kind of robot is Cyro?

A robot that resembles a jellyfish! Cyro was built by the U.S. Navy. It is the size of a beach umbrella, approximately 5.7 feet long. Cyro has a jelly-fish like dome and eight metal arms. It can be used to keep a watch over the ocean, make maps of the ocean floor and study life under water.

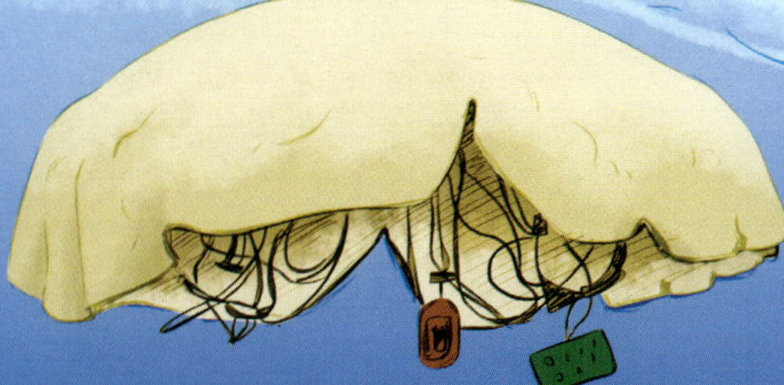

Pocket fact

The word "Cyro" comes from the Latin name of Jelly Fish, cyanea capillata.

What kind of a robot is a Robear?

It is a nursing robot! The Robear is a Japanese robot that helps elderly people or patients to sit and stand. It is said to be a "strong robot with the gentle touch" because it is strong enough to lift a person and supports them with care.

Find out

How are robots used by doctors?

RIBA

The first model of Robear was announced in 2009. It was called RIBA and later renamed to Robear.

What makes robots useful workers?

Robots can be wonderful workers because they can be used in different environments like blistering heat, freezing cold or places that are dirty! They can also explore volcanoes or be sent to far away planets where human beings cannot reach. Robots can work for days without being tired or bored!

Why?

Why do we need robots?

They do many jobs that humans cannot! A robot is a man-made machine that can perform tasks that are usually carried out by humans, either automatically or by remote control. We need robots to perform repetitive actions or some jobs that are too dangerous for us to do. They can be used underwater, sent to far-off planets and even inside our body where humans cannot reach!

Pocket fact

Biomimetics
Scientists observe the shape and movement of animals closely and copy them in a machine's design. This is called Biomimetics

Find out

What is the set of instructions given to a robot called?

Flying Robots

Snake Robots

Nano Robots

Human-like Robot

Why is every robot designed differently?

Every robot has a different job to do! The job of the robot determines what the robot looks like. For example, a robot that has to be sent into the ocean might be shaped like a fish. On the other hand, a robot that helps to lift patients in a hospital would be similar to a human being. Robots also have specific types of movement, sensors and parts based on the task they perform.

Why do robots need a power source?

Power sources make the robots work! Just as we need food to live and work, robots need a power source that helps them work. Different robots work on different power sources like batteries, solar cells and thermoelectric generators. The majority of mobile robots work on battery power. The power source completely depends on the type of task a robot performs.

Find out

What are the main parts of a robot?

Pocket fact

I am powered by air!
Some robots also use either a bottle of pressurized air or have a compressor in its body as a power source!

Why does a robot have a controller?

It works as the brain of the robot! The Controller also called the "brain" of the robot is a device run by a computer program. The controller takes inputs from us and helps the robot function in a controlled manner.

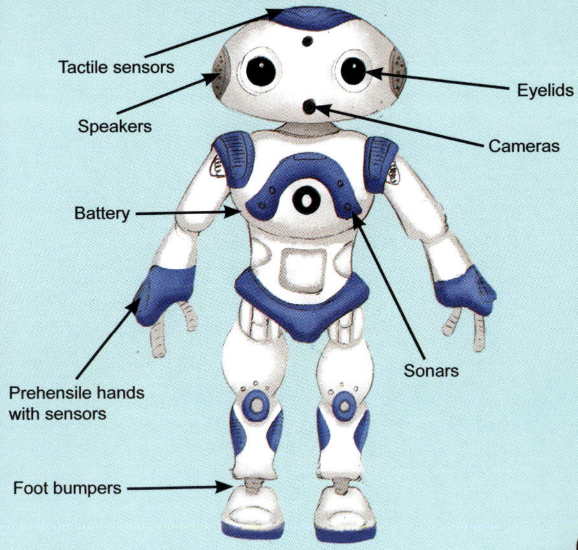

Why do robots have sensors?

They help the robots connect to the outer world! Robot sensors are parts similar to human sense organs. They help the robots to see, touch, hear, detect light and move. The robot uses the information about their environment from these sensors in order to function properly.

Pocket fact

Some robotic sensors can also detect magnetic fields which usually human beings cannot.

Find out

Do robots have touch sensors?

Why do robots need internal sensors?

To help us know the internal state of the robots! Robots are built with sensors inside their body that help us to measure their position and speed. They are also used to monitor and control the various joints of a robot.

Why are pressure-sensors used in robots?

To help them grip objects! Some robots have pressure sensors in their hands. These tell the controller of the robot how hard it is gripping a particular object. This prevents the robot from dropping or breaking whatever it is carrying.

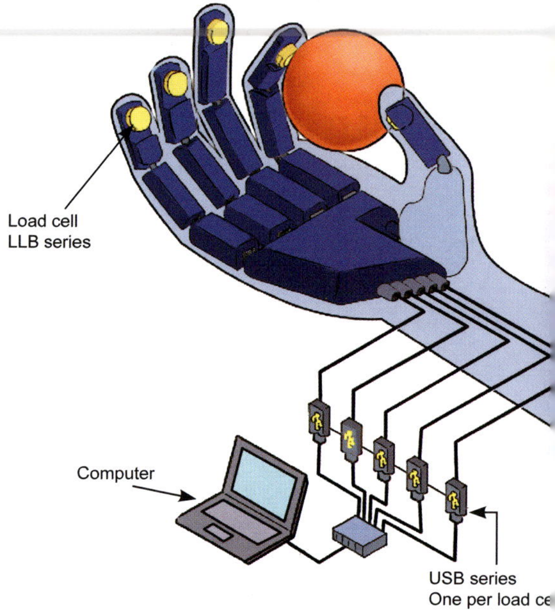

Find out

What are light sensors in a robot used for?

Pocket fact

GPS Sensors

Some robots that are placed outdoors have GPS sensors. This helps us to locate the position and speed of the robot.

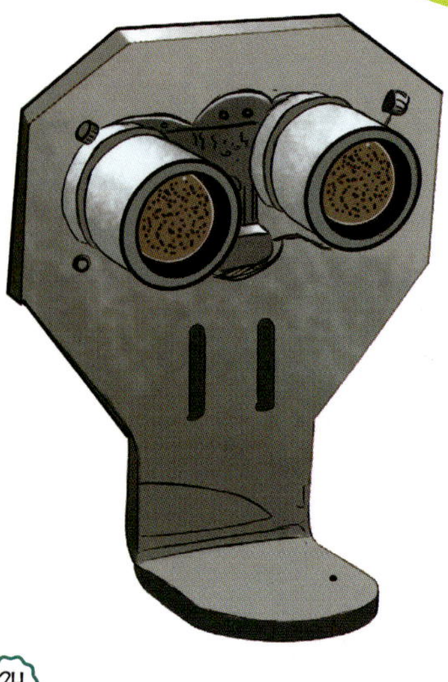

Why do some robots use ultrasound sensors?

To help them see obstacles! Ultrasound sensors in a robot work the same way as echolocation in bats. The robot sends out a sound signal or a beam of infrared light and detects the signal's reflection. This helps the robot locate how far the object is, based on how long it takes the signal to bounce back!

Why are remote robots also called puppet robots?

Such robots are controlled by remote control! Robots that are controlled by a remote are instructed what to do and when to do it by human beings and hence are called puppet robots. The remote control communicates with the robot through an attached wire, or using radio or infrared signals. Puppet robots are useful for exploring dangerous environments such as the deep sea or inside a volcano where humans can't reach.

Pocket fact

Micro controller!
A remote control robot uses a micro-controller which act as the robot's brain. It receives information from the sensors and the remote control and acts upon it.

Find out

What kind of a robot is the Urbie?

Why is a bump-and-go robot called so?

Because it has a bumper sensor! The bump-and-go robot has sensors that help it to detect obstacles. When the robot is turned on, it moves along in a straight line. On detecting an obstacle, the impact pushes in its bumper sensor. The robot's program instructs it to back up, turn and move forward again. Thus, the robot changes direction every time it hits an obstacle.

Why are mobile robots better than static robots?

Mobile robots help us in a number of ways. These explore other planets or places on Earth that are difficult for humans to reach. Mobile robots help in collecting geological samples, work in homes and businesses, transport medications in hospitals, patrol museum galleries at night, monitor air quality and humidity levels.

Pocket fact

The first mobile robots were developed between 1939-1945.

Find out

Who developed the first robotic arm?

Why are robotic arms called so?

Because it is designed like a human arm! A robotic arm is a mechanical arm that works like our arms. It is usually made up of seven metal segments. These segments are joined by six joints. Robotic arms are used in automobile industry for painting and welding auto parts. They perform different jobs and functions that are very tiring, difficult or dangerous for us to do.

Why do robotic arms have joints?

To help them move! Robotic arms closely resemble the human arm. While humans have seven joints, robotic arms have six! The robotic arm has three main parts- a shoulder, an elbow and a wrist. There are step motors connected to each joint. This allows the robot to move the arm and repeating the same movement over and over again!

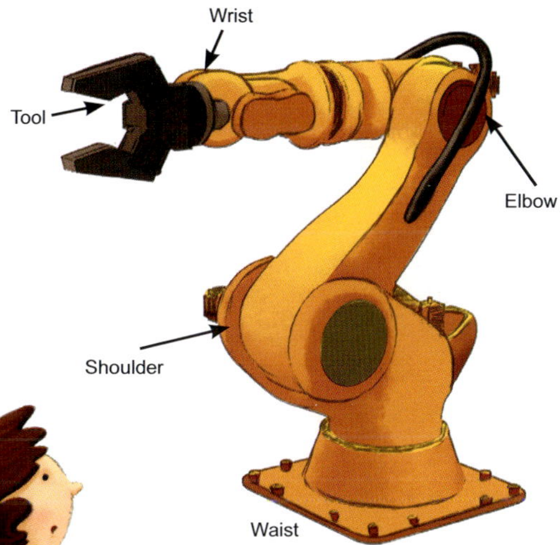

Find out

In which other industry are robotic arms widely used?

Pocket fact

The first robotic arm was developed in the 1950s by a scientist named George Devol, Jr.

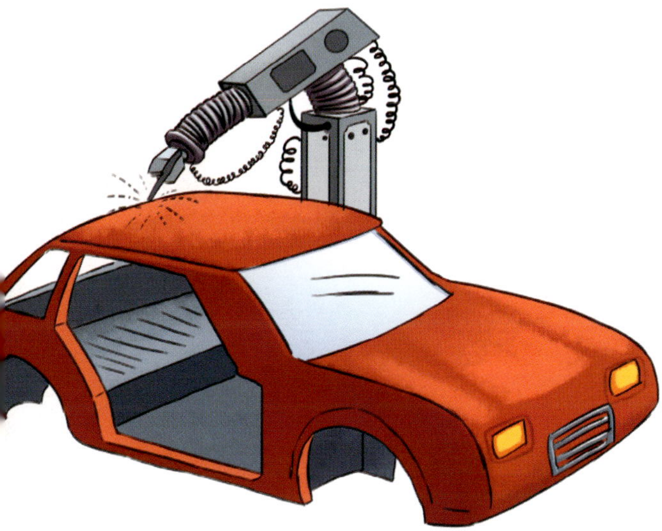

Why do car companies use robotic arms?

They can do a number of jobs! Robotic arms are widely used in car manufacturing these days. They can weld parts, paint, install windshields, mount wheels and more. Car manufacturers prefer robotic arms over humans because some of the jobs are highly repetitive. Robotic arms never tire or get distracted, so every cycle is performed the same way.

Why do robots have pistons in their legs?

They help the robots walk! Robots that are designed like humans have pistons that help them move their legs back and forth. Just like muscles are attached to different bones in our body, pistons are attached to different parts of a robot's leg. A roboticist needs to fix the right combination of pistons and program this information into the robot's computer to get the robot going!

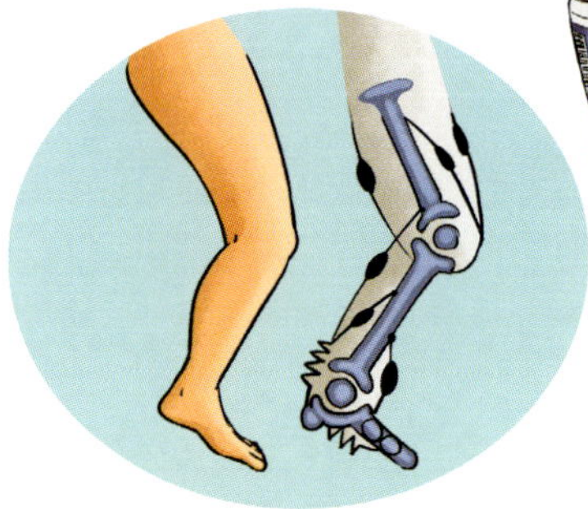

Find out

What is walking on two legs called?

Pocket fact

Help me balance!
Many moving robots have gyroscopes that help them balance and correct their movements.

Why do roboticists copy animals for robot movements?

To create more stable robots! Humans can walk on two legs easily but such movement is very unstable for robots. So engineers observe and copy the animal world, especially insects. Insects with six legs have a good balance and can be used in different kinds of environments.

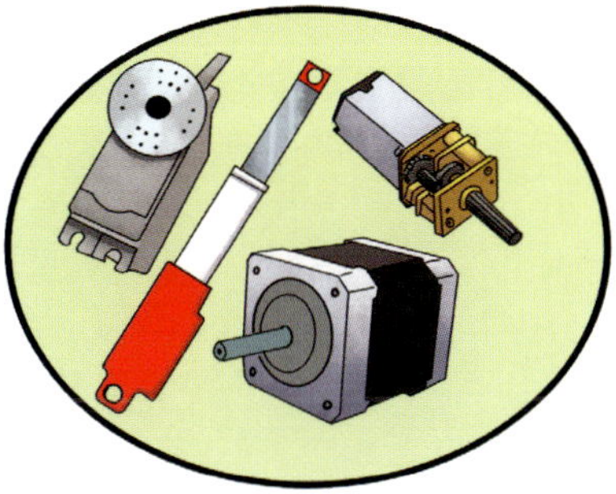

Why do robots need actuators?

To control the robot! An actuator is a part of a machine that is responsible for moving and controlling it, for example by opening a valve. It works with the help of a control signal and source of energy. When an actuator receives a control signal it converts it into mechanical motion.

Find out

How many kinds of actuators are there?

Pocket fact

Actuators are not only used in robots but also in cars. They convert electric signals from the control unit into an action.

Why do robots have a built-in balance system?

To check its movement! Many mobile robots have a built-in balance system that helps the robot balance and correct its movement. These robots usually have a collection of gyroscopes consisting of a wheel or disc. The wheel or disc can spin rapidly about an axis and is free to change its direction.

Why do robots need a program?

Robots are machines. They cannot think and act on their own, and cannot even understand human language. Just as we have machine language for computers, roboticists prepare a set of coded commands or instructions for robots. These instructions guide the robot what tasks to perform.

Find out

What kind of a robot was Blendo?

Pocket fact

A malfunction!
In 1981, a robotic arm accidentally crushed a Japanese factory worker.

Why do robots malfunction?

There can be a number of reasons! Robots are said to malfunction when they fail to function normally. This can happen when we make errors in writing robot programs. Robots also malfunction when there are errors in its software, failure of its parts, fixing wrong parts and disrupted power supply.

Why do doctors use snakebots?

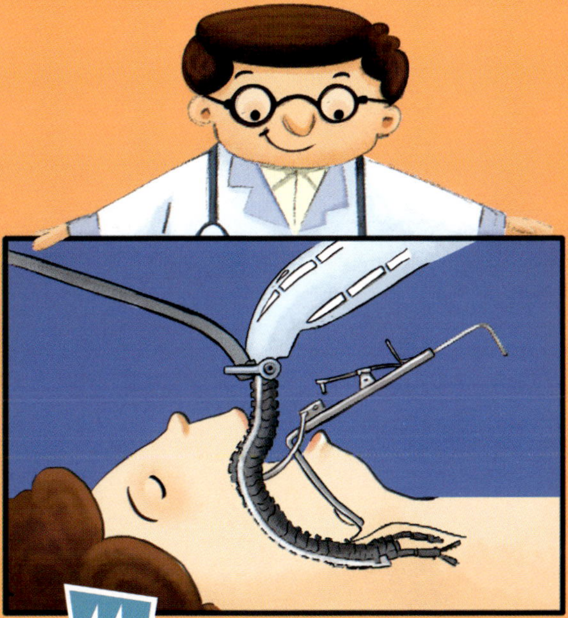

To help them in surgeries! Snakebots are robots that resemble a snake. They have a long body and can crawl from side to side. Some tiny snakebots are used by doctors to identify diseases and perform surgeries because they can curve around our organs. These snakebots carry tiny cameras, scissors and forceps, and even more advanced sensors to help the doctors!

Pocket fact

A snakebot has about 30, identical, hinge-like modules linked together in a chain.

Find out

What are the other uses of a snakebot?

Why are robots used in space?

Robots are sent to explore space for a lot of reasons. Space has many harsh conditions like high temperatures, lack of oxygen and water, high levels of radiation, etc. Robots can survive in all these conditions. They can remain and move in space for many years and can even be left on other planets, which is not possible for humans to do. Also it is much cheaper sending a robot to space than a human.

Why is a RoboTuna called so?

It resembles a fish! RoboTuna are robotic fish developed by a team of scientists in the United States. It resembles the fish tuna -one of the fastest fish in the oceans. RoboTuna can mimic the movements of the real tuna and is an ideal underwater vehicle. It swims to explore deep ocean areas and coral reefs.

Find out

When was the RoboTuna built?

Pocket fact

Ocotobot is the world's first soft-bodied robot.

Why is an Octobot called so?

It resembles an octopus! Octobot is an autonomous robot developed by a team of scientists at the Harvard University. It is made of rubbery material and no hard parts. It has eight bendy tentacles, a liquid circuit to control its movements and stretchy actuators which make its arms move. Octobot is different from other robots as it works on chemical reactions and not electricity!

Why are robots useful workers?

They can do a number of tasks without getting bored! Robots were invented so that they can help us to do a variety of jobs. Robots are very useful in factories, in space, surgeries, exploring seas and oceans and more. They can do jobs much faster than us. They can perform tasks that are dangerous or repetitive. All this makes robots useful workers for us.

> **Pocket fact**
>
> No humans!
> A factory where only robots work without the presence of human beings is called a 'light out'.

> **Find out**
>
> Who gave the laws of robotics?

Why are there laws for robots?

Robotic laws are a set of rules that are devised to protect humans from interaction with robots. There are three main laws: A robot may not injure or harm a human being. A robot must obey the orders given to it by us. A robot must protect its own existence as long as it doesn't harm humans.

How?

How are robots different from other machines?

A robot is a machine that is programmed by a computer to perform many tasks. It is an automatic mechanical device that may be in a form similar to a human or animal. In scientific usage a robot typically refers to a machine with some kind of artificial intelligence. Robots can be used for jobs like exploring space, medical surgeries, in auto manufacturing companies, etc.

Find out

What are the uses of a drone and a robot?

Pocket fact

A drone is also known as Unmanned Aerial Vehicle (UAV). It doesn't have a human pilot on plank.

How is a robot different from a drone?

A drone is a semi-autonomous vehicle that can move without human control. It is usually attached to a larger spacecraft, and to expand a ship's launching capabilities. On the other hand a robot is a machine directed by a computer program. It contains sensors, control systems, power supplies, manipulators and software all working together to perform a task.

How many kinds of robots are there?

Many different kinds! Robots can be classified in two possible ways- application and movement. On the basis of different tasks, robots can be divided into these categories- industrial, domestic or household, medical robots, service, military, entertainment robots, space robots, hobby and competition robots. On the other hand, the types of robots on the basis of movement are stationary robots, wheeled robots, legged robots, swimming robots, flying robots and swarm robots.

Try this!

Make a design of your own robot on a paper. Think what parts would you like your robot to have!

Pocket fact

The first electronic robots were built by William Grey Walter in England in 1948.

How many parts does a robot have?

A robot is made up of many big and small parts but they cannot be created without three main parts. These are the controller, the mechanical parts and the sensors. The controller acts as the brain of the computer. The mechanical parts include motors, pistons, grippers, wheels and gears. Sensors are parts that help the robot interact with its surroundings. They act as human sense organs.

How are robots made?

It involves a number of steps! The first step in making robots is making its body. Different parts are moulded, designed and assembled into a structure. After the basic structure is prepared, the roboticists write programs (set of instructions) for the robot. After the programs are written, the robots undergo inspection and testing for a number of days. When the tests are successful, robots are ready for use!

Pocket fact

Teach Pendant
Various models of the robotic industrial machinery are programmed using teach pendant. It is a handheld device and may be wired or wireless.

Find out

What is an autonomous robot used for?

How are robots programmed?

A program is a set of instructions written for a robot to perform actions. Robots are programmed using "on-line" or "off-line" methods. The online program enables the robot to perform tasks like paint, spray, pick and place objects, spot welding, machine loading and unloading. However, different robots are programmed differently according to the industry they are used in.

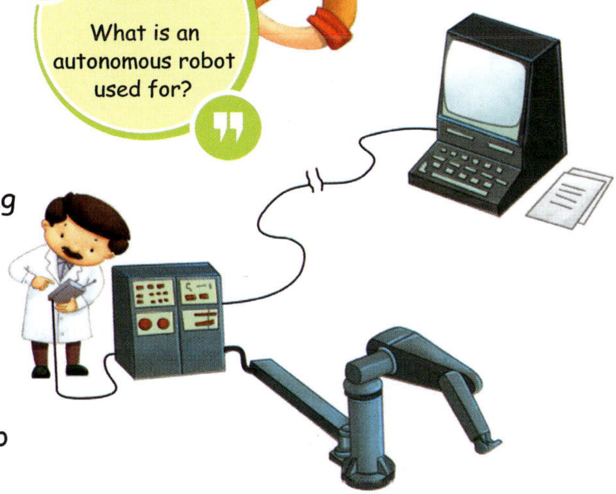

How important are actuators for a robot?

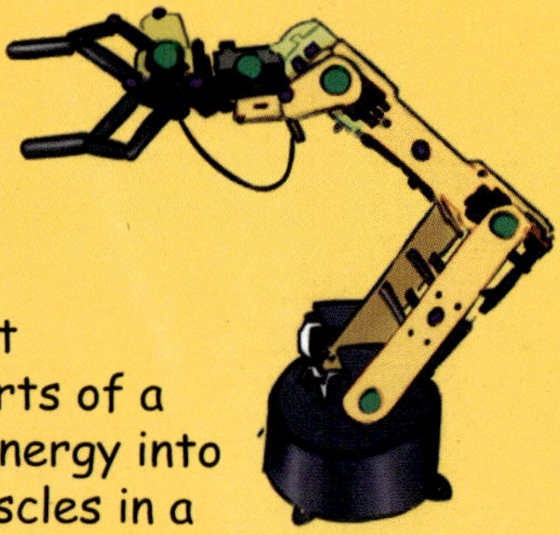

A robot cannot move without actuators! Actuators are parts of a robot that convert stored energy into movement. They are like muscles in a human body. The most popular kinds of actuators are electric motors and linear actuators. Electric motors rotate a wheel or a gear while linear actuators are used to control robots in factories.

Pocket fact

The first actuation system was created by Xhiter Anckeleman. It was for the brakes of a car to ensure maximum force.

How do robotic sensors work?

A robotic needs a lot of information about its environment to function effectively. The sensors of a robot help it to interact with its surroundings. They allow the robot to determine size, shape, feel pressure, see and hear. The robot receives the signals about the environment through its sensors. These signals are passed to the controller which tells the robot how and what to do.

Find out

How many kinds of sensors do robots have?

How are robots powered?

Robots are machines that can work tirelessly for hours. They don't need food and water; but a power source to work. The main source of power for robots is batteries. Other sources include thermoelectric generators (which convert heat directly into electricity), fuel cells and super capacitors (which store high energy on plates and tethers of a robot, which connect the robot to the power supply.

Pocket fact

The first working robot made cars as part of the production line at car giant, Ford, back in 1961.

Find out

What is a cyborg?

How do robots work?

Robots are of different types and perform different tasks. They sense the environment, plan on the action to perform in order to achieve the task and execute the planned action. Robots usually work with the help of motors and sensors. These sensors fetch information from the environment and pass it on to the controller. Based on this information the control unit is coded and gives commands to the robot on which work to do and how to do it.

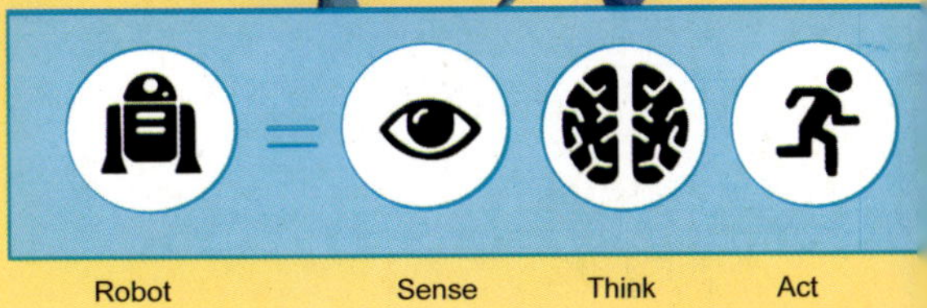

How do robots help humans?

In a number of ways! The benefits of robots are seen in productivity, safety, and in saving time and money. Today, robots are used in a wide variety of industries. Some robots help to build cars in large factories whereas some are used in modern warfare. They can do tasks that are extremely dangerous for humans to perform. Robots save time by being able to work more and faster. They are so accurate that they don't make mistakes or waste material.

> **Pocket fact**
>
> The Silver Arm is a robot arm that is capable of assembling small parts together using touch sensors.

> **Find out**
>
> Name two robots that NASA sent to space.

How can robots help the environment?

Robots have been of great use for humans in different fields. They are used to study deep-sea ecosystems, detect changes in various environmental parameters with time, aerial surveillance of protected areas, detection of wildfires, etc. Robots can also be deployed to map and assess the riverbed, as well as monitor pollution levels.

How do robots 'see' the world?

With the help of vision sensors! A robot is not a living being and hence cannot see on its own. But it has vision sensors. These are viewable objects that work in a very similar way as cameras. They act like 'eyes' and help the robot to identify their surroundings. Robots analyze the images using the sensors and act accordingly.

Find out

What is the easiest form of robotic movement?

Pocket fact

Robot GPS!
Robots can detect their exact position in space using sensors like the GPS or Global Positioning System.

How do robots move?

In a number of ways! Almost all robots have a movable body. Some have motorized wheels while others have dozens of movable parts, usually made of metal or plastic. These individual parts are connected together with joints. Robots can move these joints using actuators which are controlled by a computer.

How do robots communicate with each other?

Robots can perform complex tasks when they are linked to other machines or robots for sequence control and sensors. They communicate using binary signals, analogue signals, networks or special interfaces. Robot controllers have a range of different communication ports that can be used for various applications.

Find out

Which was the first robot to be used in medical surgery?

How do robots recognise objects?

With the help of sensors! Robots have different kinds of sensors based on the job they perform. These sensors help the robot identify objects on different parameters. One such application is the "pick-and-place" system. It is made up of a robotic arm outfitted with a custom gripper and suction cup. A program is written to allow the robot to grab an item and hold it securely without knowing anything about it beforehand.

Pocket fact

SDR-4C are robots that can remember people's faces, sing and even dance!

How do robots learn to do things?

By changing its program! When roboticists teach any robot a new task, they usually change the set of instructions (i.e the program) of the robot. This helps the robot to work in specific ways like moving to precise locations or moving things by hand. This also enables the robot to record the movements so that it can replicate them later. Humans can quickly learn complex tasks, while robots have to be laboriously taught.

> **Pocket fact**
>
> Baxter has an animated screen instead of a "face". This helps it to display multiple facial expressions.

> **Find out**
>
> What kind of robot is the Sawyer?

How is the Baxter robot different from other industrial robots?

It is a robot that learns by guidance! Baxter is an industrial robot with two arms and an animated face. It is different from other robots because it doesn't need programming and coding to work. We can teach Baxter how to perform a task by moving our hands in the desired motion and having Baxter memorise them. It has extra dials, buttons and controls for accuracy.

How did the first modern robot look like?

It was a robotic arm! The first modern robot was called the Unimate. It was invented by an American inventor George Devol. Unimate weighed 4000 pounds and was used to sequence and stack hot pieces of die-cast metal in General Motors Factory. It obeyed step by step commands that were stored on a magnetic drum.

Pocket fact

HAL (hybrid assistive limb) is the biggest achievement in robotics.
It reads brain signals and helps disabled people and the elderly to move.

Find out

Which is the most human-like robot ever made?

How are modern robots different from earlier robots?

Robots in the past were usually mechanical and did not work by programming. They were used for entertainment or day-to-day tasks like striking hour clocks. The first programmable robot was invented much later in the 1950s. Modern robots are of different kinds ranging from robotic arms to humanoids and robonauts. Today robots are used for several purposes like space exploration, teaching, research, in auto industries and much more!

How did the first computer-controlled artificial robotic arm look like?

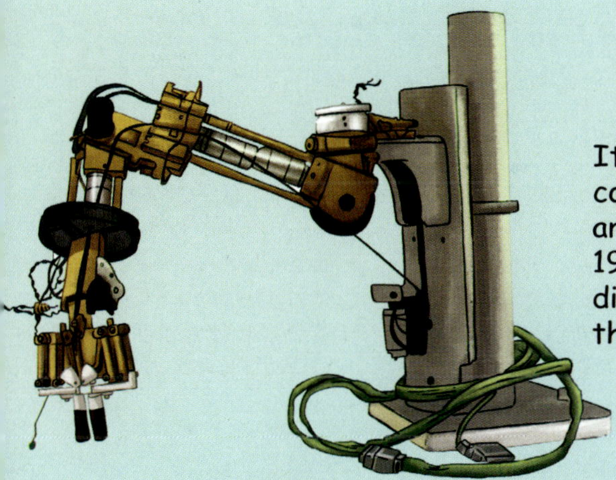

It resembled a human arm! The first computer-controlled artificial robotic arm was called the "Rancho Arm" in 1962. It was invented for physically disabled people. It had six joints so that it could work like a human arm.

Pocket fact

It is said that Leonardo displayed his robot at a celebration hosted by Ludovico Sforza at the court of Milan in 1495.

Find out

In which country was the Rancho Arm invented?

How was Leonardo's robot similar to modern humanoids?

It had a lot of common features to modern humanoids! Leonardo da Vinci designed a humanoid called the Automation Knight around the year 1495. It could stand, sit, raise its visor and move its arms. Its entire system was operated by a series of pulleys and cables.

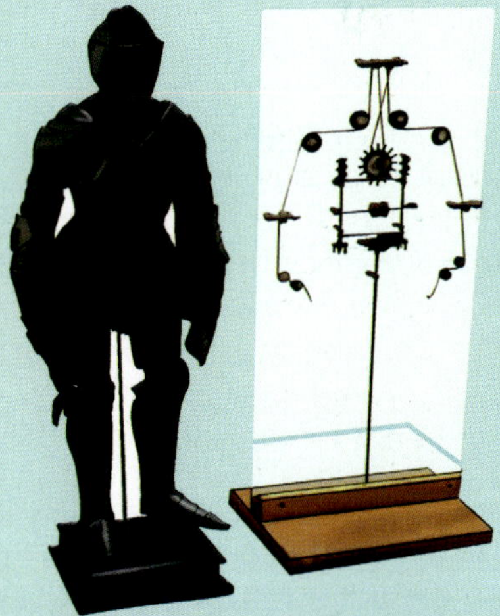

How are humanoid robots constructed?

They are designed in a way that resembles a human being in structure. A humanoid is a fully automated robot. It has a torso with a head, two arms and two legs. Some humanoid robots also have a head with eyes and mouth. They have sensors to interact with the surroundings and actuators that perform like muscles and joints, and help the robot move like we do. Humanoids are used for research in several scientific areas.

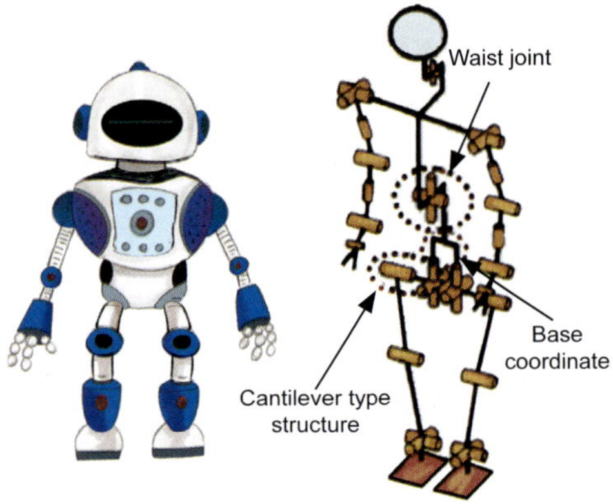

> **Pocket fact**
>
> The largest and strongest humanoid robot is Titan. It can carry engine blocks, ship and aircraft parts. and has been listed in the Guinness Book of World Records.

Find out

What kind of a robot is Sophia from Hong Kong?

How are humanoids different from other robots?

Humanoid robots are different from other robots in appearance and movement. They move like humans using two-legged locomotion. They are created in such a way that they use minimum energy while walking, as it does in the human body. Humanoid robots don't stay still like factory robots and can also detect obstacles while moving.

How are robots controlled?

In many ways! Robots are most often controlled using a wire, wirelessly or autonomously. The easiest way to control a robot is using a handheld controller connected to the robot using wires or a cable. Infrared transmitters and receivers are modes of wireless control. The third mode is to use a microcontroller in the robot to and program it so that it can receive information from its sensors and react accordingly.

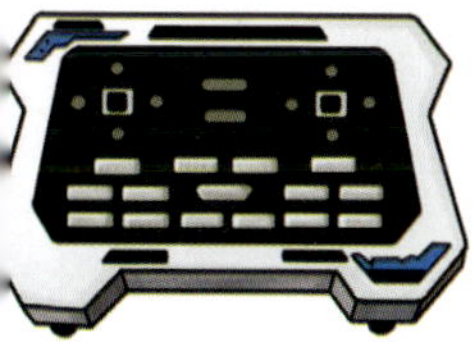

Pocket fact

A microcontroller is often called the "brain" of a robot. It allows to program a robot's behaviour.

Find out

Can robots be controlled by Bluetooth?

How does autonomous control work in robots?

Autonomous control is used in different forms: pre-programmed with no feedback from the environment, limited sensor feedback and complex sensor feedback. To control a robot automatically a variety of sensors and pre-written codes are created. This allows the robot to what action to perform in any given situation. The most complex robots currently use GPS navigation, vision systems and a variety of sensors to work.

When?

When is a machine called a robot?

A machine is called a robot when it can carry out a series of complex actions automatically. A robot is programmable by a computer and guided by an external control device. It can only perform tasks that engineers program into its computer. Each robot is designed differently based on the job it does.

Find out

What was the clock jack?

Pocket fact

The Hero of Alexandria wrote a book Automata. It is a collection of different devices which could have been used in temples thousands of years ago.

When were robot-like creatures first observed?

Long ago in the 18th century! Robot-like miniature devices were popular as toys for the rich. These looked and moved like small animals or humans. A famous creation of this time was a mechanical device "The Duck" created by Jacques de Vaucanson. It had wings with over four hundred moving parts. The duck could flap its wings, eat and even digest grain! Vaucanson also created an automated human figure that played the flute.

When was the Steam Man invented?

In 1865! The Steam Man was a steam-powered robot invented by John Brainerd. It was about ten feet high and shiny black in colour. Its face was made of iron with a pair of fearful eyes, and a grinning mouth. A whistle-like device was made to answer for the nose. The Steam Man had arm like projections and broad flat feet. It was used to pull wheeled carts!

Pocket fact

A robot called the Electric Man was invented by Frank Reade Jr. in 1885. It is more or less an electric version of the Steam Man.

Find out

What does the word robot mean?

When was the term robot first used?

In 1921! The term "robot" was first used in a play written by the Czech writer Karel Capek. The play was called "R.U.R." or "Rossum's Universal Robots". In this play, a man creates a robot to replace him but later the robot kills the man!

When was the human-like robot ELEKTRO introduced?

In 1939! The human-like robot ELEKTRO was created by the Westinghouse Electric Corporation in Mansfield between the years 1937-1938. It could walk, talk, smoke and had voice control. It was first introduced at the 1939 world's fair. ELEKTRO was seven-feet tall and weighed 265 pounds. It could say around 700 words by producing a low dull sound from a 78 rpm record player hidden behind a curtain.

Pocket fact

Sparko!
Sparko was a robot dog that joined ELEKTRO at the 1940 World's Fair. It could both bark and sit on command.

Find out

Who is called the father of robotics?

Robotics

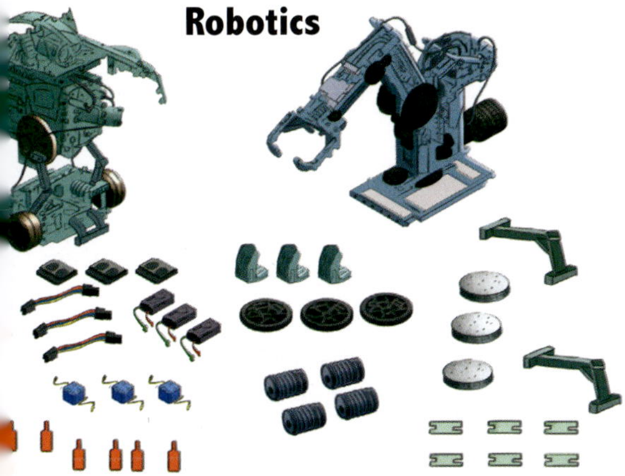

When was the word "robotics" first used?

In 1941! The word 'robotics' was first used by the science writer Isaac Asimov. It was used to describe the technology of robots. Today robotics is said to be the study and use of robots. Asimov also predicted that robotics will be a powerful industry in the future.

When was the first modern robot invented?

In 1954! The first truly programmable robot was invented by an American engineer Geroge Devol. It was called the UNIMATE short form for "Universal Automation" It was a robotic arm that could repeat a sequence of actions and was used in industries.

Pocket fact

4000 pounds!
The UNIMATE robot weighed 4000 pounds. It was controlled by vacuum tubes used as digital switches.

Find out

What was the name of the world's first robot manufacturing called?

When did the world's first robot go to work?

In 1961! The world's first robot that went to work was the robotic arm, UNIMATE. It was introduced by George Devol in a die-casting factory of General Motors in New Jersey. Its job was to remove and stack hot metal parts from a die-casting machine and weld these parts on auto bodies. The robot was quite helpful to factory workers who could be poisoned by exhaust gas or lose a limb if they were not careful.

When was the first robotic pet created?

The first robotic pet was invented by the Sony Company (Japan) in 1999. It was a robotic dog and was called AIBO. It had a beagle-like appearance and could interact with people. AIBO is a series of robotic pets manufactured by Sony. Though most models resemble dogs, there are other pets like lion cubs and space explorers.

Find out

What does the word AIBO mean?

Pocket fact

Tweet Tweet!
Robonaut sent its first tweet on 26 July 2010.

When would organizations other than NASA benefit from Robonaut?

In just a few years from now! NASA's partner, General Motors, is working towards using R2 to make its cars safer. It also hopes to use lessons drawn from R2 to make a safer work environment.

When was the El-E fetch robot invented?

In 2008! The El-E Fetch is a robot that helps people who have trouble getting around.. It is about 5.7 feet tall and has two camera eyes. El-E Fetch is automated and understands commands using a simple laser pointer. When you point the laser at any object around, the robot will run across the room, pick it up and give it to you. It can also speak, wash dishes and even clean up the entire house!

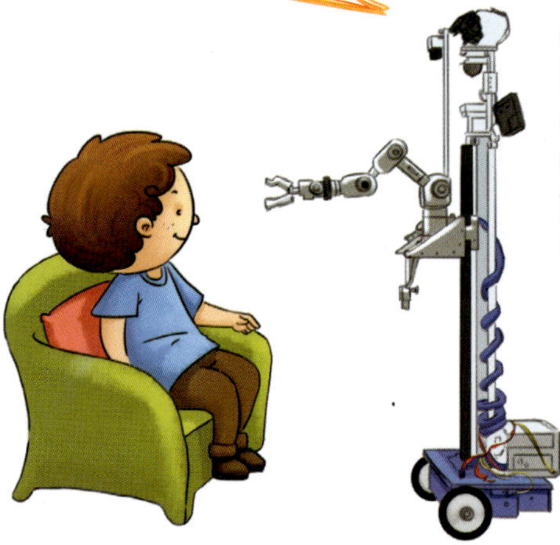

Pocket fact

The Kuratas is said to be the world's first giant robot. It was demonstrated at the Wonder Festival in Japan.

Find out

What is the full form of El-E in the name of El-E Fetch robot?

When was the world's biggest robot created?

In 2012! The world's biggest robot is the Kuratas developed by artist Kogoro Kurata and roboticist Wataru Yoshizaki in Japan. It is 4 metres high, weighs approximately 4,500 kgs and has four wheels. It can be crewed by one person. The operator sits on a seat inside the robot and controls it using the device in front of him. The Kuratas can also be controlled by a remote control.

When was the QRIO robot created?

In 2003! The QRIO was a bipedal humanoid robot developed by the Sony Company. It was 2 feet tall and weighed 7.3 kg. It was created to follow up on the success of Sony's AIBO entertainment robot. QRIO robot could recognize the voice and face. This enabled it to remember people and also their likes and dislikes!

Find out

What is the full form of ASIMO?

Pocket fact

The QRIO was originally called the Sony Dream Robot.
The full form of QRIO is Quest for CuRIOsity.

When was the ASIMO robot invented?

In 2000! The ASIMO is the world's most advanced humanoid robot and was created by the Honda Motor Company. It is 4 feet 3 inches tall. ASIMO can walk on its own, climb stairs; recognize its user's voice, face and name. It can also turn on lights, open doors, carry things, and even read emails!

When was the first biped robot created?

In 1973! The first biped robot was called the Wabot-1. It was created by Waseda University, Japan. It could walk with its lower limbs, and gripped and transported objects with hands. Wabot-1 could also measure distances and directions to objects using external receptors, artificial eyes and ears.

Pocket fact

A biped robot is the one that can walk on two legs just as we do.

Find out

Where did the HelpMate robot first went to work?

When was the HelpMate robot invented?

In 1984! The HelpMate is a mobile robot developed by Joseph Frederick Engelberger for hospitals and nursing homes. It can navigate throughout a hospital by following a map stored in its memory. HelpMate can also carry medical supplies, records and lab samples and deliver them to different hospital departments.

When were rover robots sent to Mars?

In 2003! NASA launched twin robotic rovers called Spirit and Sojourner as part of their mission to explore Mars. The Sojourner is 6 inches long, 19 inches wide, and 12 inches tall. The Spirit is 7.5 feet long, 5 feet wide and 5 feet tall. The Sojourner took 550 photographs and did some research on a rock named Yogi.

Find out

What is the other name of the rover Spirit?

Pocket fact

The first model of a robonaut was called Robonaut 1 or R1.
It head, two eyes, two arms and two five-digit hands.

When was the R2 robot sent to space?

In 2011! The R2 was sent aboard the International Space Station in 2011 and hopes to take over repetitive and dangerous tasks on the International Space Station.

When was the world's smallest and lightest robot helicopter invented?

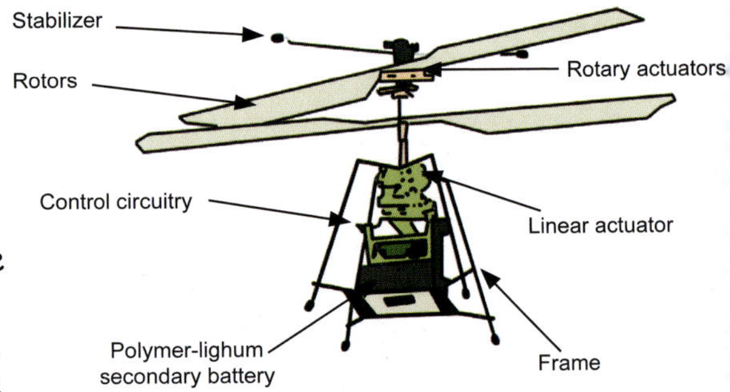

In 2003! The world's smallest and lightest robot helicopter model is the Micro Flying Robot. It was developed by Seiko Epson to explore the possible use of micro robots. It has two microprocessors, Bluetooth, a gyro-sensor and image sensor. The robot is powered by an external battery through a power cable and thus cannot fly high.

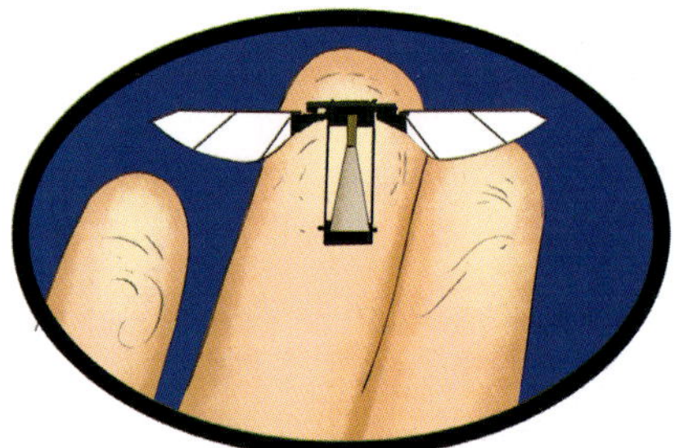

Find out

Which is the world's smallest microrobot?

Pocket fact

The Big Dog can walk in snow and water, climb muddy hiking trails, and carry up to 150kg loads.

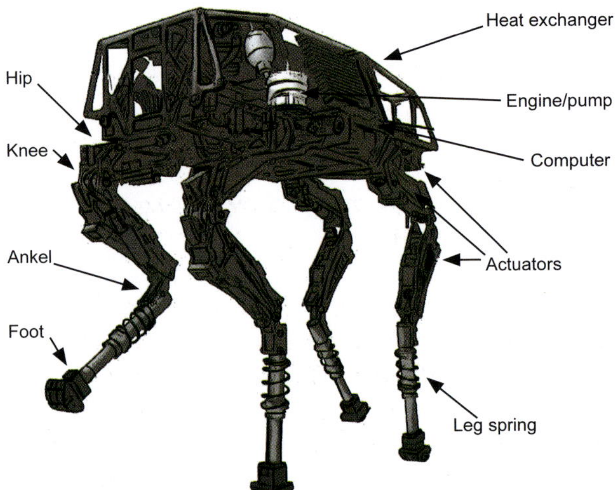

When was the Big Dog robot invented?

In 2005! The Big Dog is a four-legge military robot created by Boston Dynamics. It is 3 feet long and 2.5 fe tall about the size of a small mule. It doesn't have wheels, instead uses its legs to follow a person and move safe around rocks and trees. The Big Dog was invented to accompany soldiers i rough lands where conventional vehic cannot be used.

When was the ACTUV robot ship invented?

In 2010! The ACTUV is a robot ship invented by the US Navy. It is designed to track submarines for up to 90 days at sea. It is in constant contact with other ships and aircraft through a satellite link. If there's no threat, a sailor can order the robot to go back on patrol.

Pocket fact

The Actroid robot can talk to a group of people and also handle if someone interrupts it while talking.

Find out

What is a female Android robot called?

When was the Actroid robot created?

The Actroid is a humanoid robot created by Osaka University, Japan. Its skin is made of silicone and looks like a young Japanese child. Actroid has speech recognition software. It can copy basic human functions and can talk and blink. It was introduced at the 2003 International Robot Exhibition, Tokyo.

When was the Zeno robot invented?

In 2007! Zeno is a humanoid robot boy developed by a team from Imperial College London to interact with children who have autism. It is 17 inches tall and weighs 4.5 pounds. Its prototype was displayed at the 2007 Wired Nextfest. Zeno is said to be an intelligent "conversational robot" that will teach autistic children how to understand and convey their emotions.

Pocket fact

Zeno teaches in a fun way. It plays games, shows pictures, tells stories and asks the children to describe what they see!

Find out

How many kinds of robots are there?

When does a robot get tired?

Never! A robot is a machine that can be designed for working continuously It doesn't need food and water like humans. It can work without getting bored and tired. All we need to make sure is to provide the robot with a correct set of instructions and powe it with an electric outlet or battery s that they can work efficiently.

When can a robot stop working?

When you run a robot beyond its operation time! Robots are machines that should be inspected and maintained regularly. Most robots have a fixed period of operating time. Robots may stop working after those fixed hours. They also don't work when there is cable damage, the software is corrupt or they lose their ability to smoothly perform actions repeatedly.

Find out

What should we do to prevent robot malfunctions?

Pocket fact

Most industry robots have a 3,840 hour period of operating time.

When does a robot malfunction?

There are many reasons! A robotic malfunction occurs when it behaves differently- smashing and destroying things. This can occur due to a lot of reasons like errors in program, control panels, a failure in the power source or even wrong installation of its equipment.

Index

OTHER TITLES IN THIS SERIES

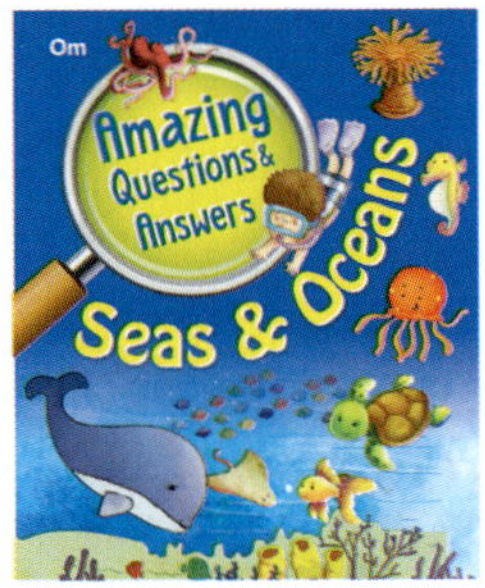